ALL THOSE TOUGH
EXPERIENCES IN YOUR
LIFE HAVE BEEN THERE
TO BRING YOU TO WHERE
YOU ARE RIGHT NOW...

1

HOW TO ENJOY THE GOD STUFF

Written and
Illustrated by

HUGH CLAYCOMBE

David C. Cook Publishing Co.
850 NORTH GROVE AVENUE • ELGIN, IL 60120
In Canada: David C. Cook Publishing (Canada) Ltd., Weston, Ontario M9L 1T4

3811

To my father
who took me upon his knee
when I was a small boy
and taught me how to draw.

CONTENTS

*YOU'RE ONLY MAKING THAT MUCH MONEY?
YOU MUST NOT BE VERY VALUABLE!*

THEY'RE LOOKING AT ME!
THEY'RE TALKING ABOUT ME!

I CAN'T TRUST ANYBODY.

THEY HAVE EVERYTHING.

THEY'RE OUT TO <u>GET</u> ME!

I NEED EVERYTHING THEY TALK ABOUT
IN FILMS AND MAGAZINES. IT'S
THE ONLY WAY I CAN STAND UP TO THEM.

14

BUT I DON'T HAVE IT.

IT'S NOT THAT I WANT TO WIN POPULARITY
CONTESTS... I JUST WANT TO FEEL
<u>WORTH</u> SOMETHING.

YOU'RE WORTH *EVERYTHING* TO ME.
THAT DAY OF MY *SUFFERING*
    I AGONIZED OVER YOU.

ALL THOSE TOUGH
EXPERIENCES IN YOUR
LIFE HAVE BEEN THERE
TO BRING YOU TO WHERE
YOU ARE RIGHT NOW...,
TO BRING YOU TO ME.

19

YOU ARE <u>UNIQUE</u>.
  THERE'S NO ONE LIKE YOU.
    THERE'S NEVER BEEN ANYONE LIKE YOU.

HE SAYS I'M UNIQUE. HE SAYS I MEAN
SOMETHING TO HIM. BUT WHY DO THINGS BUG
ME DEEP DOWN INSIDE? WHY DO I
NEED TO KEEP UP MY TOUGH IMAGE?

MY SPIRITUAL RECEIVING INSTRUMENT
IS SO BADLY WRECKED THAT I'M UNIQUE
ALL RIGHT... A UNIQUE FAILURE.

Chapter 2.
DO I REALLY NEED CHURCH?

I DON'T LIKE CHURCH.
IT SEEMS TOO MUCH LIKE A
LAUNDROMAT WHERE PEOPLE
PAY THEIR QUARTER, GET
WASHED AND DRIED, THEN GO
BACK OUT AND GET
ALL MESSED UP AGAIN.

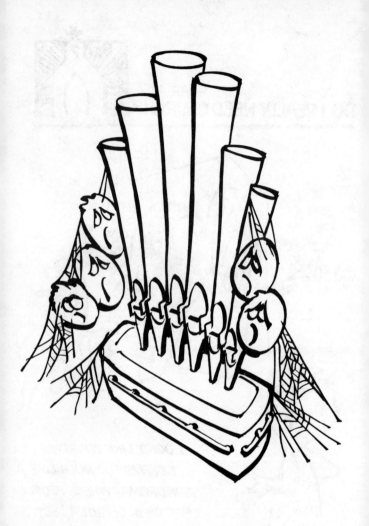

FORMAL LITURGY SEEMS LIKE A DIRGE.

BUT JAZZ, FOLK AND ROCK
SERVICES ARE EVEN WORSE.

ANOTHER THING, IT'S HARD TO SEE THE
REAL PEOPLE BEHIND THE CHURCHY
LANGUAGE THEY USE.

27

YUK! A BUREAUCRATIC CHURCH.

IT SEEMS THAT WITH SOME PEOPLE WHAT THEY
SAY THEY BELIEVE IS MORE IMPORTANT
THAN WHAT THEY ACTUALLY BELIEVE.

THEIR WORDS BLOCK OUT
ALL COMMUNICATION WITH GOD.

THE
FEUDING
CHURCH

THE SOCIETY
CHURCH

SUCH AN ASSORTMENT OF
CHURCHES! CAN I EXPERIENCE
THE GOD STUFF IN
ANY OF THEM?

32

THE
COMMITTEE
CHURCH

THE BUILDING-
FUND CHURCH

THE LAZY CHURCH

THE OLD MAID CHURCH

THE DEAD CHURCH

THE EXPECTANT CHURCH

THE "WE'RE THE ONLY ONE" CHURCH

THE FRIENDLY CHURCH

MAYBE MY _OWN_ LIFE
COULD USE A REPAIR JOB.

37

I'VE BEEN LOOKING ONLY AT THE CHURCH,
INSTEAD OF AT JESUS AND THE CROSS.
BUT WHO CAN UNDERSTAND THE CROSS?

ANCIENT MAN, I'M CONFUSED. YOU SAY "THE BLOOD OF JESUS CLEANSES US FROM SIN." YOUR LANGUAGE IS OBSOLETE. EVERYONE KNOWS BLOOD IS MADE UP OF CORPUSCLES. WE MAKE IT INTO PLASMA.

LOOK, 20TH CENTURY MAN, TO US FIRST CENTURY JEWS THE _LIFE_ OF A CREATURE IS IN IT'S BLOOD.

OUR WORSHIP
DEMONSTRATED
THIS. HERE YOU SEE
US BRINGING A LAMB
FROM OUR FLOCKS...
A PERFECT AND
INNOCENT
CREATURE.

THE HEAD OF A
HOUSEHOLD WOULD
PLACE HIS HANDS ON
THE LAMB'S HEAD,
TRANSFERRING TO IT
THE SINS OF HIS
ENTIRE FAMILY.

OUR RABBI MADE A TINY CUT IN THE LAMB'S NECK
AND ITS BLOOD WAS DRAINED. BUT MORE THAN
BLOOD, THIS INNOCENT LAMB POURED OUT HIS
ENTIRE LIFE... AND WITH IT THE SINS
OF OUR ENTIRE FAMILY.

OUR PRIESTS POURED THE BLOOD UPON THE BASE
OF THE ALTAR IN THE JERUSALEM TEMPLE.
GOD RESPONDED TO OUR OBEDIENCE BY POURING
OUT HIS FORGIVENESS UPON US.

SO IT WAS WHEN
JESUS, THE CHRIST, POURED OUT
HIS BLOOD FROM THE CROSS... WE WHO ACCEPT
HIM as OUR MESSIAH SAW HIM as POURING
OUT HIS VERY SOUL..., HIS _SPIRITUAL_ SELF...
ALL THAT WAS WITHIN HIM... FOR US!

YOU WON'T FIND A VICTORIOUS LIFE BY JUST
SHOPPING FOR A PERFECT CHURCH. IT COMES BY
ACCEPTING _HIM_. THEN YOU'LL BECOME A
PART OF HIS REAL CHURCH... WHICH IN YOUR
CENTURY IS GOING THROUGH SOME CHANGES.

SOME PEOPLE ARE BEING DRAWN
TOGETHER TODAY BY THE HOLY SPIRIT.

PEOPLE ARE BECOMING INTERESTED IN JESUS
AND THE SPIRIT FILLED LIFE INSTEAD OF
CHURCH POLITICS,

PRAYER AND BIBLE STUDY GROUPS ARE SPRINGING UP ALL OVER. NEW TRANSLATIONS AND PARAPHRASES MAKE GOD'S WORD COME ALIVE.

BOOKS ON PRAYER AND RENEWAL ARE APPEARING EVERYWHERE... EVEN IN THE SUPERMARKETS... AND THEY'RE SELLING FASTER THAN CAKE MIX!

LOTS OF THINGS ARE CHANGING.

49

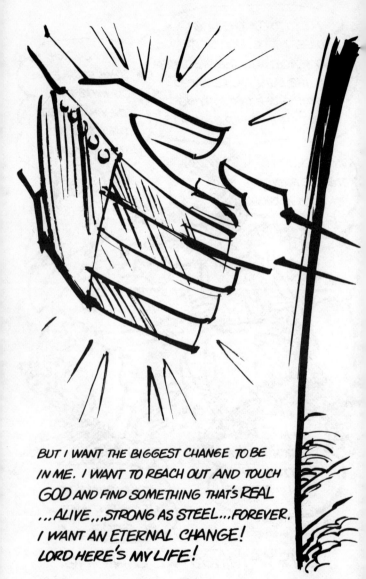

BUT I WANT THE BIGGEST CHANGE TO BE
IN ME. I WANT TO REACH OUT AND TOUCH
GOD AND FIND SOMETHING THAT'S REAL
...ALIVE...STRONG AS STEEL...FOREVER.
I WANT AN ETERNAL CHANGE!
LORD HERE'S MY LIFE!

50

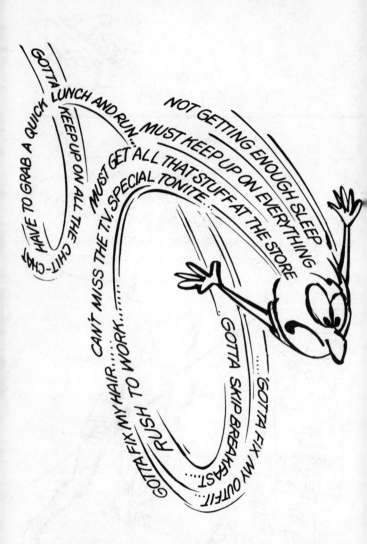

I SHOULD SPEND SOME TIME GETTING TO KNOW
YOU NOW, LORD, BUT I'M ALWAYS ON THE GO.

MAYBE I COULD SNIP OUT SOME TIME FOR PRAYER.
MAYBE JUST A LITTLE BIT AT FIRST...
BUT I'LL DO IT REGULARLY, <u>AT THE SAME
TIME</u> AND <u>PLACE</u> EVERY DAY!

ALL THIS STUFF IS DUE ON
RUN OVER TO THE ST...
CAN'T STOP DOIN...

FINISH UP WI...
NO TIME FOR T...
MUST DO MORE
WORK IS DUE D...

THE QUIET ZONE

HURRY
PROJECTED
SCHEDULE:
WILL HAVE TO
RUSH DOWNTOWN...

NOTHING IN THIS WORLD
LETS ME STOP FOR 3 MINUTES
JUST TO BEHOLD THE GLORIES
OF GOD. IT TAKES
INGENUITY!

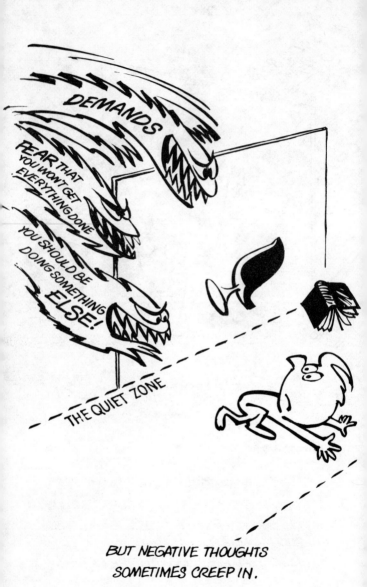

BUT NEGATIVE THOUGHTS
SOMETIMES CREEP IN.

WHO EVER SAID THEY WOULDN'T?
MY SPIRIT WILL DESTROY THEM IF YOU LET
HIM. BY THE WAY, YOU USED TO FIND TIME
TO FACE YOUR PROBLEMS WITHOUT ME,
REMEMBER?

59

IT'S TRANQUILITY TIME... MY COCKTAIL HOUR.

ALCOHOL ENABLES ME TO RELAX, SO MY MIND IS CLEAR... TO THINK ... THOUGHTS.

MY COCKTAIL HOUR FLOATS MY MIND AWAY FROM ALL MY PROBLEMS.

BUT UGH... THE NEXT DAY....

MANY PEOPLE HAVE TROUBLE PRAYING. HERE'S A
TIP. TRY THE INNER SPACE TRANQUILITY TEST. TURN
OFF ALL MUSIC, T.V., AND RADIOS. STOP ALL TICKING
CLOCKS. STAY AWAKE AND LISTEN TO THE SILENCE.
FLUSH OUT YOUR MIND. CAN YOU LIVE WITH THAT
SELF THAT IS STRIPPED CLEAN FROM ALL OF LIFE'S
DISTRACTIONS? GOD LOVES THAT SELF.

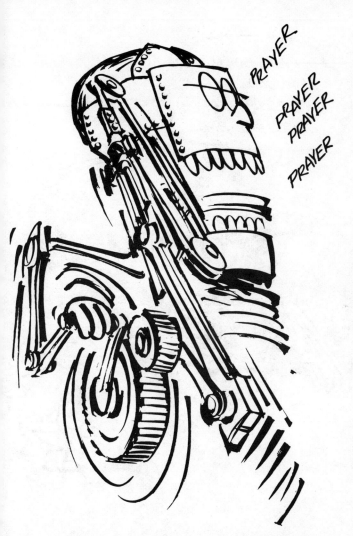

PRAYER

PRAYER
PRAYER

PRAYER

SOME PEOPLE HAVE TROUBLE PRAYING BECAUSE
THEY TURN IT INTO A MECHANICAL EXERCISE.

OTHERS HAVE NEVER PROGRESSED BEYOND
THE POINT WHERE THEY FIRST STARTED.

SOME PEOPLE ENDED THEIR
EXPERIMENTS IN PRAYER LONG AGO.

SOME OF US ARE RATHER
EMBARRASSED TO TALK ABOUT GOD.

69

YOU'LL FIND HE'LL CHANGE YOU INTO A RECEIVING
INSTRUMENT, NOT JUST A SENDING ONE.

THIS GUY IS ON THE ROAD TO SUCCESS.
NOTHING STANDS IN HIS WAY.

THE WORLD CALLS THIS GUY A LOSER.

STOP YOUR THOUGHTS!

I MUST BOMBARD THE MINDS OF MILLIONS OF AMERICANS WITH MY T.V. COMMERCIAL

YOU MUST SWITCH TO MY BRAND

SO THAT A FEW OWNERS OF MY COMPANY CAN GET RICH

BOY, AM I GLAD
I DON'T LIVE IN <u>YOUR</u> COUNTRY...
THEY FILL YOUR MIND WITH PROPAGANDA
ALL DAY LONG!

HOW CAN I FORGET ABOUT
MATERIALISTIC STANDARDS?

I'LL LOOK AT THINGS GOD HAS MADE.
LIKE THE OAK TREES DOWN ON THE CORNER.
THEY'VE ALWAYS BEEN THERE.

79

THE SWINGERS ALWAYS SEEM
TO HAVE SUCH A TERRIFIC LIFE!

THEY'VE GOT A SWINGING DEATH, TOO!

THE TROUBLE WITH MATERIALISM
IS THAT IT CAN TAKE YOU WITH IT!

Chapter 6.
THE CHRIST THRUST

ME vs. YOU!

I GOTTA WIN!

*I'VE BEEN TAUGHT THAT
IF I DROP MY OFFENSIVE THRUST,
I'LL GET SMASHED.*

BUT I CAN TAKE CHRIST
AS MY BUSINESS PARTNER.

I CAN EMPTY MYSELF OF THAT
OLD "THRUST OF SELF" MENTALITY.

ANYONE CAN BECOME A
CHANNEL THROUGH WHICH THE
LOVING QUALITIES OF GOD FLOW.

Chapter 7.
THE REAL SELF

PEOPLE HAVE A WAY OF LABELING US.

SOMETIMES WE ACTUALLY BELIEVE
THAT THESE DESCRIPTIONS ARE
OUR REAL SELVES.

DON'T WE WISH PEOPLE WOULD UNDERSTAND
US AS WE _REALLY ARE_... _DEEP DOWN INSIDE?_

JESUS DOES. THE REAL SELF IS SPIRITUAL.

HE NEVER BOUGHT THOSE SUPERFICIAL LABELS.

IF OUR TRUE IDENTITY IS SPIRITUAL, THEN WE ARE
HERE SIMPLY TO REFLECT THE QUALITIES
OF OUR LOVING AND ETERNAL GOD!

FORGET ABOUT THE CROWD.
PICK ONE PERSON AND TRY TO SEE THE
SPIRITUAL PERSON JESUS SEES.

LOOK PAST THE SURFACE TO THE REAL
SELF. THERE'S SOMEONE SPECIAL THERE.

YOU MAY FIND A PERSON WHO NEEDS HELP.

LORD KNOWS HOW I EVER GOT TO THIS. WILL I EVER GET OUT? WILL PEOPLE ACCEPT ME?

QUESTIONABLE

JUST LOOK AT THEIR PAST LIVES!

HOW CAN YOU COMPLAIN ABOUT ANOTHER
PERSON'S PAST WHEN I'M WILLING
TO IGNORE YOURS?

BUT THEY'RE
ALL WRONG!

LET ME BE THE
JUDGE OF THAT.

I LOVE EACH OF THEM SO DEARLY.
HOW CAN YOU DO LESS?
MAYBE YOU ARE NOT WILLING TO SEE
THAT THEY ARE CAPABLE OF
REFLECTING ME.

IN EACH OF THOSE MILLIONS
OF HOMES ARE VERY SPECIAL LIVES.
YOUR HEAVENLY FATHER LOVES
EACH LIFE SO DEARLY.
YOUR CAN TOO.

TRY ACCEPTING EACH HOME AS SPECIAL.
EACH LIFE AS PRECIOUS. EACH PERSON
AS BEAUTIFUL IN HIS OWN WAY. SEE HOW
WARM AND _SMALL_ AND _FRIENDLY_
THIS _BIG_ WORLD CAN BECOME!

ALL THIS TRAFFIC, YET IN EACH CAR
ARE HUMAN BEINGS...
EACH ONE PRECIOUS TO GOD.

THAT MAKES THE RUSH HOUR CROWD
DIFFERENT, DOESN'T IT?

BUT LEAVE THE BURDEN OF JUDGMENT
UP TO ME. IT WILL FREE YOU UP TO LOVE
PEOPLE AND TO ENJOY THE GOD STUFF!

Chapter 8

USING THE GOD STUFF

IT'S MONDAY MORNING.

BUT I'VE STILL GOT THE GOD STUFF.

A ROTTING LEAF.

LIFE IS ROTTEN. WINTER IS COMING.

A BEAUTIFUL LEAF.
LIFE IS BEAUTIFUL. SPRING WILL COME.

NOT MUCH TIME LEFT.
AND EVERY YEAR GETS WORSE.

SO MUCH TIME AHEAD.
AND IT'S GETTING BETTER.

THE TRUTH IS, NOW MY LIFE IS AN
INSTRUMENT THROUGH WHICH
THE GOD STUFF FLOWS TO OTHERS!

I WILL CALL UP SOME OF MY DEAR FRIENDS
AND TELL THEM HOW MUCH GOOD HAS COME
INTO MY LIFE JUST BECAUSE THEY'RE ALIVE...
THAT I LOVE THEM AS _GIFTS_ FROM GOD!

THAT'S ONE WAY TO ENJOY THE GOD STUFF!

Chapter 9

THE LAND OF
ANSWERED PRAYER

*I'VE COME A LONG
WAY BUT IT'S BEEN
NO PICNIC.*

AM I UNWILLING TO ADMIT THAT GOD HAS LED ME
ALL THIS WAY? THAT HE HAS HEALED ME? THAT HE
HAS DECLARED MY PAST AS CLEAN? AREN'T ALL
OF THE BLESSINGS THAT I NOW HAVE
    THE REALITY OF ANSWERED PRAYER?

WHY SHOULD I PUT MY
FAITH INTO NON-GOD?

123

NOW I LIVE IN THE LAND OF ANSWERED PRAYER. EVERYTHING REFLECTS THE BEAUTY OF GOD!

GOD CHANGED ME
INTO A PERFECT RECEIVING
INSTRUMENT OF HIS LOVE.
I PRAISE HIM FOR IT.